*Be strong and take heart, all you
who hope in the Lord.
Psalm 31:25*

**The intent and
purpose of this volume is to
give you faith, hope and inspiration.
Hopefully it will help bring peace and
tranquility into your life. May it be a
reminder of God's love, guidance
and His many blessings.**

**Our publications help to support our work
for needy children in over 130 countries
around the world. Through our programs,
thousands of children are fed, clothed,
educated, sheltered and given
the opportunity to live
decent lives.**

Salesian Missions wishes to extend special thanks and gratitude to our generous poet friends and to the publishers who have given us permission to reprint material included in this book. Every effort has been made to give proper acknowledgments. Any omissions or errors are deeply regretted, and the publisher, upon notification, will be pleased to make the necessary corrections in subsequent editions.

First Edition Printed in the U.S.A. by Concord Litho Group, Concord, NH 03301.

Hope for a Brighter Tomorrow

from the
Salesian Collection

Compiled and Edited
by Jennifer Grimaldi

Illustrated by
Russell Bushée, Paul Scully,
Robert VanSteinburg, Bob Panteleone,
Terrie Meider, and Dorian Lee Remine

Contents

Reflect on the precepts of the Lord, let His commandments be your constant meditation; then He will enlighten your mind, and the wisdom you desire He will grant.
Sirach 6:37

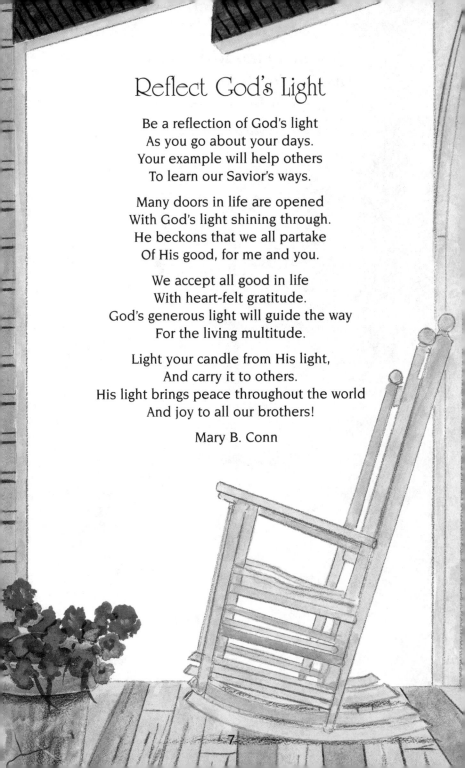

Reflect God's Light

Be a reflection of God's light
As you go about your days.
Your example will help others
To learn our Savior's ways.

Many doors in life are opened
With God's light shining through.
He beckons that we all partake
Of His good, for me and you.

We accept all good in life
With heart-felt gratitude.
God's generous light will guide the way
For the living multitude.

Light your candle from His light,
And carry it to others.
His light brings peace throughout the world
And joy to all our brothers!

Mary B. Conn

Lord, do not withhold Your compassion from me; may Your enduring kindness ever preserve me.
Psalm 40:12

The Garden of Life

Life is like a garden,
Whate'er we sow we reap,
So let us plant in earnest
Stout seeds of kindness deep.

May we add compassion,
Concern and tender care,
And never nurture ugliness
Or selfishness, despair.

Instead plant seeds of goodness,
The ones of joy and love,
Cast out tares of unconcern,
While lifting thoughts above.

Life's garden that's well-tended
Will produce a bumper crop,
One of many blessings,
With yields to never stop.

Virginia Borman Grimmer

Let us not grow tired of
doing good, for in due time
we shall reap our harvest, if
we do not give up.
Galations 6:9

Comfort

Dear Lord, when I am sick or tired
And heavied by my plight,
I come to You with arms outstretched,
In You I seek the light.
I've searched down many avenues
And wandered many roads
To find a place where I could dump
The burdens of my soul.
In valleys I have sought the calm
And climbed the mountains high;
But neither gave me answers sought –
I left them with a sigh.

I talked to one and talked to all
But no one gave relief.
In overwhelming sadness
I wallowed in self-grief.
Finally I came to You,
Put problems at Your feet.
You merely picked me up, dear Lord,
Your loving arms so sweet.
And now that I have shared with You
The fullness of my heart,
I know that when I walk with You,
You'll never from me depart.

Ruthmarie Brooks Silver

It's Not Always What I Want, Lord

It's not always what I want, Lord,
That is best for me.
What dreams I feel would fulfill –
God might not agree.

My vision now is finite
And I can't see beyond the bend,
But God is of the infinite
And He knows just what to send!

We may ask for sunshine and rainbows
And oft grumble and complain,
When God permits a certain trial
And allows a bit of rain.

He knows when we need virtues,
Like patience, trust, and loyalty,
But sometimes we must be humbled
Before we enter a life of royalty.

It's not always what I want, Lord,
That is best for me.
So please mold me, gracious Father,
Into what "You" want me to be!

Linda C. Grazulis

God's Rose Garden Land

There's a lovely rose garden,
God's rose garden land,
Where roses are blooming
On every hand.
There are roses of red,
Bright yellow, soft pink;
Tangerine petals, too,
Flowers fit for a king.
Amidst this rose garden
A brook wends its way;
Close by, in the meadow,
Wild roses hold sway.
Over rose arbours high
The sweet roses climb
And 'round weathered trellises
Roses entwine.
Through this lovely rose garden
I stroll every day;
Be it morning or evening,
The beauty's the same.
In June or December
Fresh roses I find,
For this lovely rose garden
Is etched in my mind.

Loise Pinkerton Fritz

The Garden of
Our Hearts

We are but tiny, little seeds
That are scattered upon this earth,
To praise and glorify our God
From the moment of our birth.

As we advance in wisdom and grace
And in His love and peace,
Somehow we gain the knowledge
That His love will never cease.

Our tears supply the moisture
That help to make us grow
In understanding and compassion
For those whom we love and know.

Our joy supplies the sunshine
That helps us to blossom strong
And gives us the power and will
To right our every wrong.

Our hearts are beautiful gardens
That are made by our God above
And every day we grow with Him
Through the abundance of His love.

Shirley Hile Powell

God's way is unerring; the Lord's promise is tried and true; He is a shield for all who trust in Him.
Psalm 18:31

Trusting

When eastern skies start to pale
After night is done,
Birds begin to twitter,
Stirring one by one.

And as the first rays appear,
They lift their heads to praise
And thank their dear Creator
For this new, blessed day.

They have no fears or concerns
Of what may come to pass.
This day is provided for;
The future's in His hands.

Teach me, dear Father, to be
More like Your blessed birds:
Serving You in this day
And trusting in Your words.

Steven Michael Schumacher

By Faith We Live

By faith we know without a doubt,
Although we cannot see,
That there's a God who cares for us,
Who gives us hope for what's to be.
By faith we trust the universe
Was formed at God's command,
And accept His Word as truth –
Unafraid to take a stand.
By faith we live to please Him
And bring glory to His name;
By faith we walk the narrow path
That we might bring no shame.

By faith we gladly give our wills
To the Savior of mankind
Who bore the cross of all our sin
And died that we might find…
Salvation in His perfect plan
And the peace and joy He brings;
For when by faith we live in Him
Our hearts can truly sing.

Sharon Fuqua

The maker of Heaven and earth,
the seas and all that is in them,
Who keeps faith forever.
Psalm 146:6

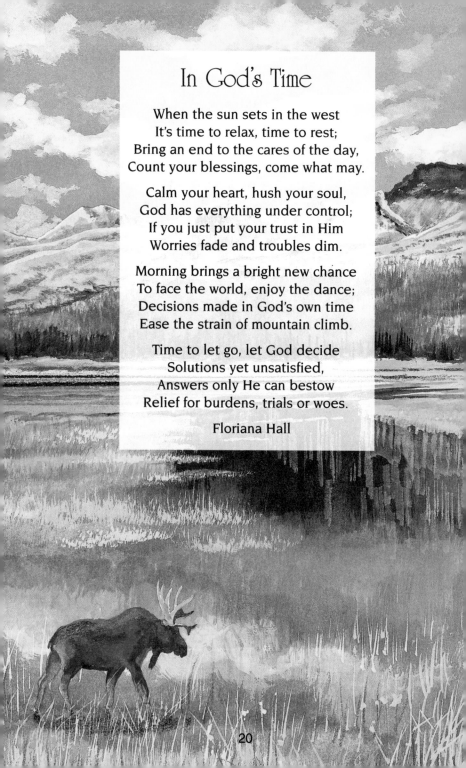

In God's Time

When the sun sets in the west
It's time to relax, time to rest;
Bring an end to the cares of the day,
Count your blessings, come what may.

Calm your heart, hush your soul,
God has everything under control;
If you just put your trust in Him
Worries fade and troubles dim.

Morning brings a bright new chance
To face the world, enjoy the dance;
Decisions made in God's own time
Ease the strain of mountain climb.

Time to let go, let God decide
Solutions yet unsatisfied,
Answers only He can bestow
Relief for burdens, trials or woes.

Floriana Hall

Secure in God's Love

God's love is sure and steady;
It will sustain day by day.
We can abide in Jesus' love
When earthly love drifts away.

No power can separate us
From God's tender loving embrace;
We can always remain in this closeness
Until we see Him face to face.

We can rest in God's affection
While we feel His mighty power.
He gives peace, joy and blessings
That arrive like a Summer shower.

The Word of Christ has promised
We are safely secure in His love.
When we become His children,
Our destination is Heaven above.

Frances Culp Wolfe

*Trust in the Lord and do
good that you may dwell in
the land and live secure.*
Psalm 37:3

The Words of Jesus

I trust my Lord and Savior,
And Jesus is His name;
I trust His Words and promises
For they remain the same…
The same today, and tomorrow;
His Words comfort each day.
They teach, and guide and shelter
And show me the right way.
The way, according to Jesus,
Is to love, without fail;
His love protects daily
From every stormy gale.

His Words say to love others;
Show love, and kindness, too.
I will try to follow Jesus
In all I say and do.
When I request forgiveness,
Because I sometimes fall,
His Words comfort my sadness
And faith makes me stand tall.
I trust my Lord and Savior;
He's with me through all strife.
I believe the Words of Jesus,
And His gift of eternal life.

Barbara Lott

When Clouds Descend

When clouds descend, dear Jesus,
Oh, may I take Thy hand;
That I might stand on solid rock,
And not on sinking sand!

Oh, help me care, dear Jesus,
For all who need my aid;
That they might seek the love of Thee,
And never feel afraid.

Oh, may I, gentle Jesus,
Forever cling to Thee;
To share Thy love with all mankind,
That blinded eyes might see.

Sancie Earman King

God, Our Lighthouse

As the little light
Goes 'round and 'round,
It offers direction
Without a sound.
In some areas
We thought were gray,
It casts its light
And shows the way.
How encouraging,
To always know,
That this beam of light
Will always show…
A brighter side,
A safer way,
To live our lives,
And save the day.

Anna M. Roos

*The name of the Lord is a
strong tower; the just man
runs to it and is safe.*
Proverbs 18:10

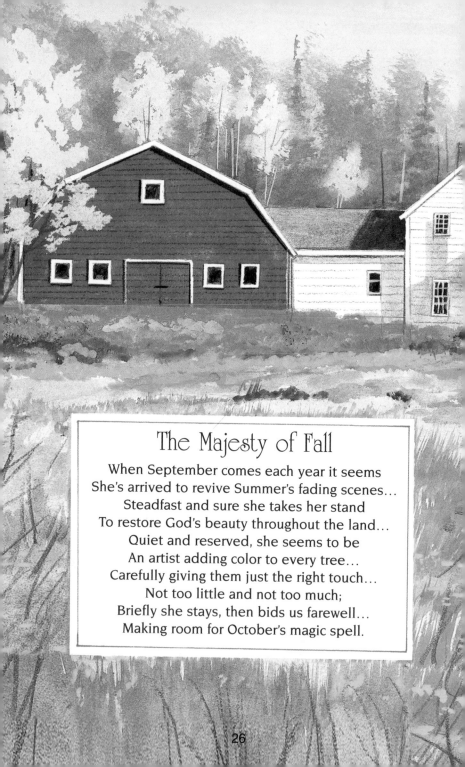

The Majesty of Fall

When September comes each year it seems
She's arrived to revive Summer's fading scenes...
Steadfast and sure she takes her stand
To restore God's beauty throughout the land...
Quiet and reserved, she seems to be
An artist adding color to every tree...
Carefully giving them just the right touch...
Not too little and not too much;
Briefly she stays, then bids us farewell...
Making room for October's magic spell.

October appears in all her fanfare,
Greeting folks with a little nip in the air…
Announcing the arrival of an early Fall,
As we hear overhead the wild geese call.
She's splashing her colors here and there
Through fields of grain and trees everywhere…
Colors more vivid now, bright and bold,
All that our eager hearts can hold…
Though we wish she could forever remain;
We welcome November's time to reign.

Lou Ella Cullipher

Nature's Cathedral

I went into the woods today
Where Autumn's glory was on display,
And then there was magic in the air
And a sense that God was there;
Maple leaves floating in the brook,
A memory etched in Autumn's book.

Oak leaves dance upon the breeze
As sunlight filters through the trees.
They fluttered by around my face
Then fell to earth in silent grace.
I memorized each sight and sound
To celebrate the peace I found.

I lingered there in silent prayer
Warmed by God's love and tender care,
In His cathedral of the trees
Where I had fallen on my knees.
God's majesty was on display
When I worshipped in the woods today.

Clay Harrison

Consider this: whoever sows sparingly will also reap sparingly, and whoever sows bountifully will also reap bountifully.
2 Corinthians 9:6

A Day in September

Wispy white clouds high in the sky,
Without haste are wandering by,
Sailing like ships in the endless blue;
A familiar sight, yet it seems always new.
The restless wind sings in the trees
His haunting, age-old melodies.
A chirping bird, a cricket calls;
And here and there a red leaf falls.
Daylilies glow in the mellow sun –
It feels like Summer has only begun.
But signs of Autumn are seen all around,
Little green apples dot the dry ground.
Noisy blackbirds have gathered again
In fields where the farmer is reaping grain.
In my heart I tuck this mild Autumn day,
Knowing its splendor will soon fade away.
And when across meadows Winter winds blow,
I pause to remember, God made it so.

Regina Wiencek

Adorn yourself with grandeur and majesty, and array yourself with glory and splendor.
Job 40:10

Autumn Arrayed in Gold

Autumn casts a golden glow
O'er the countryside,
As the green of summertime
Quickly takes its flight.
Golden are the marigolds
And the fields of grain,
Grain a-waving in the breeze,
Gold-leaved country lanes.

Varied mums of floral gold,
Golden-kerneled corn;
Golden sun rays touching earth
On an Autumn morn.
Harvest moon with golden beams...
Scenes of priceless worth.
Autumn sheds a golden glow,
A touch of Heaven on earth.

Loise Pinkerton Fritz

You made the moon to mark the
seasons, the sun that knows the
hour of its setting.
Psalm 104:19

The Silence of the Snow

The hummer's hum is silent now;
There's no buzzing of the bees,
No honk of geese in Autumn skies,
No songbirds in the trees.

The meadow is a wonderland
Of newly fallen snow,
A shimmering sea of custard
In the moonlight's afterglow.

The spruce and pine are frosted now,
And the cobwebs too,
As silently the seasons change
At Nature's rendezvous.

At dawn's first light, a brand new world
Is waiting to be seen,
A world of crystal palaces
In an ever-changing scene.

The garden's an ice sculpture now
Where roses used to grow,
A somber dream awaking from
The silence of the snow.

Clay Harrison

35

God Knocking

I knocked when the wind
Of adversity blew
And longed to pilot you
Safely through.
I knocked when your heart
Was bowed down with grief
And yearned to bring you
Sweet relief.
I knocked when your life
Lay tattered in shreds
And wanted to help you
Pick up the threads.
I knocked yet again
When you were near despair
And waited in vain
To hear your prayer.
I've knocked many times,
You have heard Me, I'm sure,
Yet still keep Me waiting
Outside the door.
I won't force an entrance
But long to come in
To give you new life
And sweet peace within.

Rosemary J. Tivey

A World of Miracles

I asked God for a miracle
So I would know that He,
The Master of the Universe,
Was still aware of me,
And that He heard my daily prayers,
Took note of my devotion,
Sent my plea, waited patiently,
Filled with deep emotion.
Within my heart, an answer came
To look around and see,
Great miracles are everywhere,
That's how I came to be!

Each life in any shape or form,
Each bit of scenery;
The sun and moon, the stars and all
Are gifts to you and me.
The seasons and the elements,
The very air we breathe;
He made this world of miracles –
A treasure to bequeath.

Betty Lou Hebert

Strength

Whenever it feels just like
My whole world is caving in,
I can find the strength I need
In the sweet promise of Him
Not to leave or forsake me,
Though the world may turn its back,
By trusting my Good Shepherd,
There is nothing I will lack.
For from the deepest sorrow
Comes an even deeper peace
He gives to us when our pain
Into His hands we release.

Steven Michael Schumacher

Just Because You're There

Each day offers me a simple choice
Of placing all within Your care
Or facing all my fears alone
With uncertainty everywhere.

Help me give those cares to You,
Help me stop to say that prayer.
Show me how to place my trust in You
All along life's thoroughfare.

When the two of us are handling
What before I could not bear,
May I often stop to thank You, Lord,
Just because You're there.

Barbara Joan Million

*But may all who seek You rejoice
and be glad in You. May those
who long for Your help always
say, "The Lord be glorified."*
Psalm 40:17

Wintertime

Wintertime is a special time
To show how much God cares,
By sending snow to cover things
So they won't look so bare.
He clothes the trees that have no leaves;
He makes them look brand new,
And diamonds seem to sparkle
With sun-rays shining through.

42

He seems to give our special earth
Some extra time to rest,
So springtime can replace it
And birds can build their nests.
God also gives the rivers rest,
Frozen deep with ice and snow,
Just waiting for Spring to come
So they can start to flow.
Yes, wintertime is a special time
For God to show He cares,
By taking time to spend with Him
In blessings we all share.

Bonnie J. Knapp-Lyons

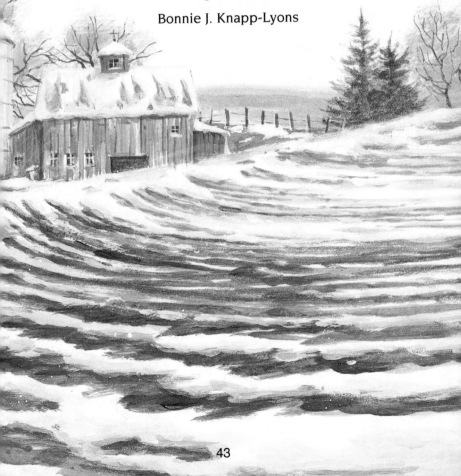

Affirmation

I'm grateful for the Winter sun
Whose shine is like a smile to me,
For birds have left the cold behind
As leaves departed from each tree.
All creatures went until the Spring
To stay as warm as they could be,
And Nature bids the earth to sleep
With only barren land for us to see.
But I know that God has kept the sun
To show He's still with you and me!

Eva Marie Ippolito

44

Winter Wonderland

I saw a Winter wonderland
Through my window late last night;
Everything was covered in a blanket of snow –
Oh! What a beautiful sight.

From a bright full moon
Snow sparkled in its light,
Not a car tire or footprint
Spoiled the lovely sight.

Pure white snow kept falling
Silently covering everything;
It's a silvery wonderland,
To my heart such joy brings.

God who made this great world
Be it day or dark of night,
Must have made the snow
Just for our delight.

Bernice Laux

*I will delight and rejoice in
You; I will sing hymns to
Your name, Most High.*
Psalm 9:3

More precious than gold is health
and well-being, contentment
of spirit than coral.

Sirach 30:15

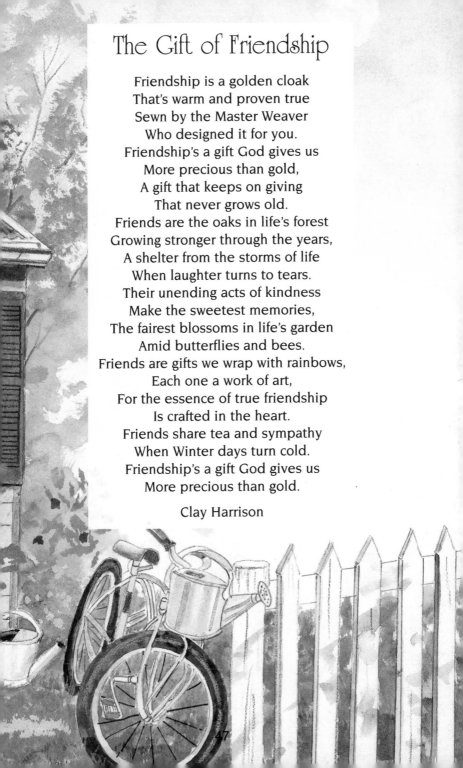

The Gift of Friendship

Friendship is a golden cloak
That's warm and proven true
Sewn by the Master Weaver
Who designed it for you.
Friendship's a gift God gives us
More precious than gold,
A gift that keeps on giving
That never grows old.
Friends are the oaks in life's forest
Growing stronger through the years,
A shelter from the storms of life
When laughter turns to tears.
Their unending acts of kindness
Make the sweetest memories,
The fairest blossoms in life's garden
Amid butterflies and bees.
Friends are gifts we wrap with rainbows,
Each one a work of art,
For the essence of true friendship
Is crafted in the heart.
Friends share tea and sympathy
When Winter days turn cold.
Friendship's a gift God gives us
More precious than gold.

Clay Harrison

Step by Step

Step by step with Jesus,
He will lead the way…
Little steps or larger steps,
We step along each day.

Sometimes just a little step
To change the manner how
We'll discard old habits,
We hope to do it now!

Jesus has great patience;
He knows we may be weak
To satisfy our yearnings
As victory we seek.

We must have endurance,
O, may our faith not stray.
Step by step with Jesus –
He will lead the way.

Edna Massimilla

*When you walk, your step will
not be impeded, and should you
run, you will not stumble.*
Proverbs 4:12

My Victory Garden

I have a victory garden,
It's planted in my heart;
It is a spiritual garden
Of which God is a part.
Salvation's in this garden
And righteousness is, too;
Prayer's also in this garden,
To name but just a few.
I have a victory garden,
It's planted in my heart;
The yield's victorious living
Since my God is a part.

Loise Pinkerton Fritz

A Smile

It's the measure of a smile
That makes a happy day,
When sunshine lights the darkness
And chases stars away.
It's at these joyous moments
When we lift up praise to God –
The love He puts inside our hearts
Is measured wide and broad.

It's the measure of a smile
That we pass to humankind
With a measured drop of happiness
In their cup of joy, refined.
It's at the joyous moment
When they see Jesus in our eyes,
And understand the Word of God,
Not wickedness and lies.

Nancy Dodrill

Gladden the soul of Your servant;
to You, Lord, I lift up my soul.
Psalm 86:4

Sharing His Love

The Lord's love is always there
For all God's creation to share.
In all strangers whom we meet,
And in those we lovingly greet.

We find it in the pounding sea;
In the unfolding of a tree.
We share it in the deep, blue sky;
In the flight of a butterfly.

Flowers in His love are rooted
With tints that are softly muted.
Springing forth in gay profusion,
Creating Heaven's sweet illusion.

The wind, the rain, the stars above
Are all signs of His undying love.
Beauty given without payment;
All adorned in His sweet raiment.

With harvests of unending food,
Giving to us all that is good,
He feeds our body and our soul;
And in our lives, He plays His role.

Dorothy Ivan Manzlak

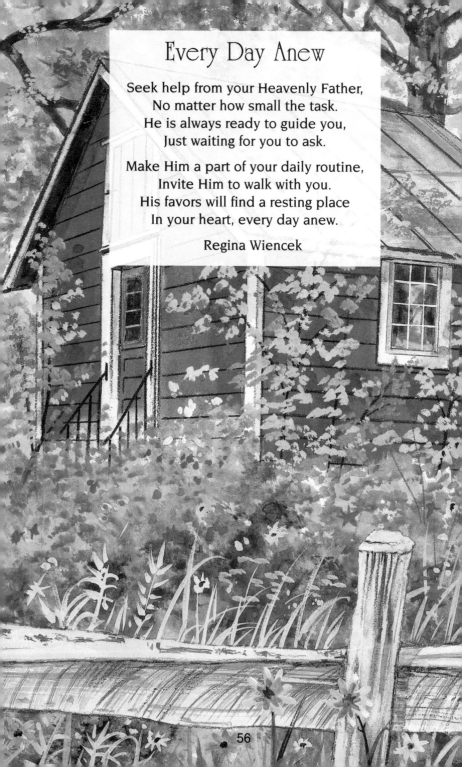

Every Day Anew

Seek help from your Heavenly Father,
No matter how small the task.
He is always ready to guide you,
Just waiting for you to ask.

Make Him a part of your daily routine,
Invite Him to walk with you.
His favors will find a resting place
In your heart, every day anew.

Regina Wiencek

Nature's Rewards

Come along and stroll the mountains
Where the ancients have walked before.
We'll behold the majesty of Nature –
Bond firmly with God's great outdoors.

We'll feel the breeze tousle our hair,
Watch the cottony clouds sail by.
Our hearts will soar with the red-tailed hawk
And commune with its plaintive cry.

All cares of the heart will vapor,
As mist from a Summer shower.
We will feel God's enveloping presence –
And know of His awesome power.

He will touch the rocks of the ages,
Smell the fragrance of delicate flowers.
To know we are one with Nature,
We will linger for hours and hours.

We will pause at a high promontory
To absorb all that Nature affords.
In reverence to God's abiding love,
We give thanks for Nature's rewards.

Charles Clevenger

From Tragedy to Triumph

From tragedy to triumph
Can be the story of our life;
For life's trials, we must go through
Our share of toil and strife.

But we can be the victors,
Our faith can take us through
To soaring heights of victory
He's prepared for me and you.

So, friend of God, do not despair
When valleys you must face;
Remember that He's with you
And we're saved by His grace.

Someday all trials will vanish,
Never more to us appear,
If we'll believe His promises
And to His Word adhere.

We'll live with Him in glory,
In mansions built for us,
His blessing to enjoy
If we in Him will trust.

Helen Gleason

*He brought His people out with joy, His
chosen ones with shouts of triumph.*
Psalm 105:43

A Soft and Quiet Stillness

A soft and quiet stillness
Begins to touch my heart.
It overwhelms my senses
And overcomes my thoughts.
This moment is accepting,
Embracing earth and sky.
I pray the Lord will bless me
And keep me safe tonight.

John Zurn

Live Life to the Fullest

God wants us to be happy
And some purpose fulfill.
We must break unhealthy habits,
This is our Father's will…

Obey His great commands,
Love God with all your heart,
And your neighbor as yourself –
This is a perfect start.

As we seek God's blessings,
Walk the narrow way.
Live life to the fullest –
Our joy will surely stay.

Edna Massimilla

*However, take care and be earnestly
on your guard not to forget the
things which your own eyes have
seen, nor let them slip from your
memory as long as you live, but
teach them to your children and to
your children's children.*
Deuteronomy 4:9

You restore my strength. You guide me along the right path for the sake of Your name.

Psalm 23:3

God Is Guiding Me

Life's road is but an unknown path –
The way I cannot see;
But I'll not fear this unknown path
For God is guiding me.

He leads me with an unseen hand –
By faith, He lights the way.
His grace is all sufficient
For my journey day by day.

I need but start the day with Him
In fellowship and prayer –
Then as I travel down life's road
I'll always find Him there.

Shirley W. Langley

But I pray to You, Lord, for the time of Your favor. God, in Your great kindness answer me with Your constant help.

Psalm 69:14

God's Blessings

As we gather round the table,
We bow our heads in prayer
To thank You, Lord, for loving us
And for Your constant care.

We thank You for our houses,
Our friends and families.
We thank You for Your guidance
And for Your perfect peace.

Thanks for all Your blessings,
The big ones and the small,
Especially for Jesus
Who gave His life for all.

Frances Gregory Pasch

But I pray to you, Lord, for the time of
Your favor. God, in Your great kindness
answer me with Your constant help.
Psalm 69:14

The Master Painter

Each Fall God takes His paintbrush
And paints an Autumn scene…
A dab of red, a touch of gold
And luscious shades of green.

Each day He adds another hue
For all the world to see.
Behold His awesome canvas!
Observe His majesty.

Frances Gregory Pasch

66

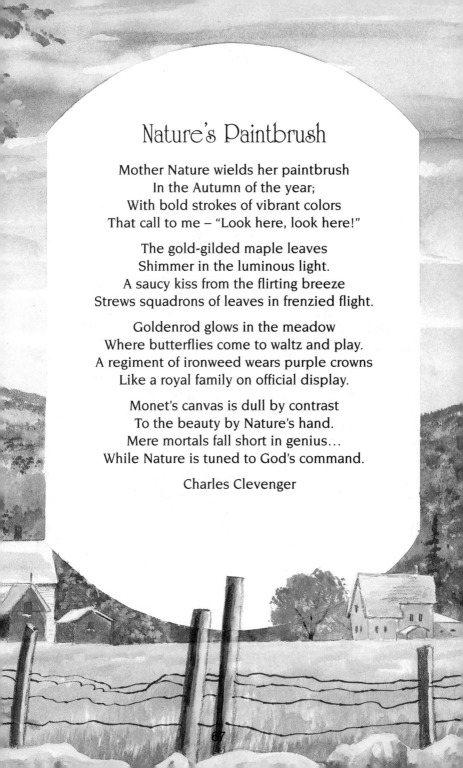

Nature's Paintbrush

Mother Nature wields her paintbrush
In the Autumn of the year;
With bold strokes of vibrant colors
That call to me – "Look here, look here!"

The gold-gilded maple leaves
Shimmer in the luminous light.
A saucy kiss from the flirting breeze
Strews squadrons of leaves in frenzied flight.

Goldenrod glows in the meadow
Where butterflies come to waltz and play.
A regiment of ironweed wears purple crowns
Like a royal family on official display.

Monet's canvas is dull by contrast
To the beauty by Nature's hand.
Mere mortals fall short in genius…
While Nature is tuned to God's command.

Charles Clevenger

Autumn Hues

Autumn leaves, the wind blows by,
Once hung beneath a clear blue sky;
Orange, russet, red and gold
Are the colors I behold.

Fall's festival of falling leaves
Mother Nature guarantees;
Cooler days are on the way,
Colors are changing day by day.

Autumn's days are short and sweet
With flying colors lying at my feet;
When God changes the scenery, all
To welcome a grand and glorious Fall.

Nora M. Bozeman

Blessed be His glorious name forever;
may all the earth be filled with the
Lord's glory. Amen and amen.
Psalm 72:19

Will I Be Ready?

Oh, will my heart be ready
To meet Jesus face to face?
Will I be able to stand
In the presence of His grace?
I know He is merciful,
But also holy and just;
Though I'm a helpless sinner,
In His Sacred Words I trust.
It will be an awesome day
When I meet God's only Son,
And I long to see Him smile
When my journey here is done.

Steven Michael Schumacher

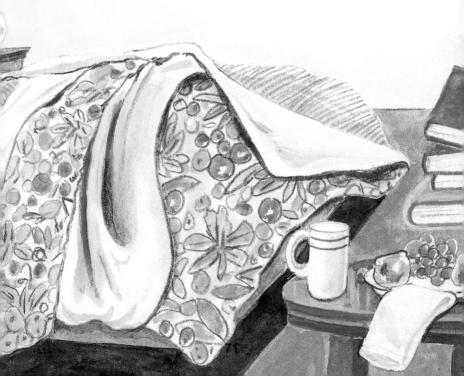

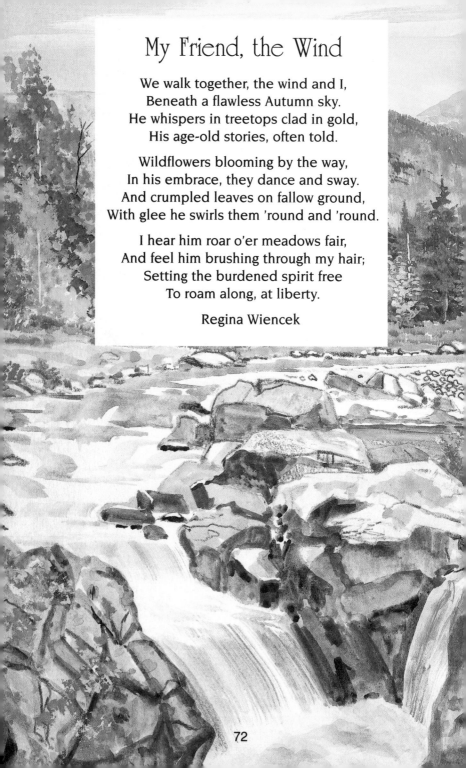

My Friend, the Wind

We walk together, the wind and I,
Beneath a flawless Autumn sky.
He whispers in treetops clad in gold,
His age-old stories, often told.

Wildflowers blooming by the way,
In his embrace, they dance and sway.
And crumpled leaves on fallow ground,
With glee he swirls them 'round and 'round.

I hear him roar o'er meadows fair,
And feel him brushing through my hair;
Setting the burdened spirit free
To roam along, at liberty.

Regina Wiencek

September Song

It seems that Summer's fading fast
And autumntime is here;
The leaves all turn to red and gold
About this time of year.

October's just a breath away
And now September song;
There's loveliness about the earth
And birds sing all day long.

The crimson red and gold and green
All to the eye will please;
Folks come from miles to mountains high
To view this lovely scene.

I thank You, God, for all I see
So picturesque and clear;
Each pretty leaf we see today
Is in Your loving care.

Katherine Smith Matheney

*The Lord is my strength and my
shield, in whom my heart trusted
and found help. So my heart rejoices;
with my song I praise my God.*
Psalm 28:7

November Is a Vagabond

November is a vagabond
In scarlet-gold attire
As the trees reflect God's glory,
Every leaf a tongue of fire.
From the woodlands to the meadows,
Nostalgia's on display
And all throughout the countryside
The scent of new-mown hay.

Roadside orchards offer cider,
Gourds and pumpkins galore
And bunches of Indian corn
To hang upon your door.
November is a gypsy spirit
For "nothing gold can stay."
All too soon Autumn's artwork
Will pale and fade away.

In these lovely fleeting moments,
Sweet memories are made
That will warm us in mid-Winter
When snow clouds promenade.
Autumn leaves renew my faith
Consumed by flameless fire.
November is a vagabond
In scarlet-gold attire.

Clay Harrison

In this you rejoice, although now for a little while you may have to suffer through various trials.

1 Peter 1:6

Only for a While

Leaves are floating on the breeze,
Leaving bare the hardwood trees.
Softly landing on the ground,
Colors quickly turning brown.
Flocks of birds southward go,
Heralding soon, the coming snow.
The woodchuck and the chipmunk too,
Preparing to sleep the Winter through.
Flowers maturing into seed,
All my Winter friends to feed.
I shiver, dressed in my Winter coat,
As fallen leaves on chilled waters float.
I feel a sadness deep within,
For all the beauty that has been.
As a tear rolls down my cheek,
I can hear the Creator speak…
His words cause my heart to smile
When He says, "It's only for a while."

Katherine Byars

If I say: I will forget my
complaining, I will lay aside my
sadness and be of good cheer.
Job 9:27

Peace

The Lord's peace, soft as a cloud,
Invades my very being,
Enveloping me in a shroud
Of a soft and airy feeling.

Light as a feather, I soar
Through mists of daily care.
No task, today, a heavy chore,
For in my heart His peace I share.

Dorothy Ivan Manzlak

Snow Melt

I cannot wait for Spring to come
To melt away the snow,
To see the green of leaves push through
Where budding crocus grow.

When soon the small birds will appear
And greet the warm Spring air,
The scent of flowers waft in the breeze,
Trees no longer bare.

Spring days will grow warmer
As trees and grass grow green;
The view outside my window,
A lovely springtime scene.

For Winter is cold and lonely,
The days pass slowly too;
Spring sometimes comes so slowly
There is nothing much to do…

As I sit here by the window
Waiting for the Spring,
Watching for the snow to melt
And to hear the robin sing.

Milly Patzer

God is my witness, whom I serve with my spirit in proclaiming the gospel of His Son, that I remember you constantly.
Romans 1:9

Memories

Deep within my memory chest
Are stored the things that I like best;
A Summer day and star-filled night,
And a snowy day with Winter's bite.

A garden filled with roses fair
Where lilacs' fragrance lingers there.
An Autumn morn with colors blast
That disappears all too fast.

A home filled with love and cheer
And family that I hold most dear.
A church where God's spirit dwells,
Where steeple holds the ringing bells.

A sunrise that makes the earth aflame,
A walk down a country lane.
When the sun sets at close of day,
I lock my happy memories away.

Shirley Hile Powell

*I will remember the deeds of
the Lord; yes, Your wonders
of old I will remember.*
Psalm 77:12

Snowflakes

The slowly blowing winds
Embrace falling snowflakes,
Escorting them to earth
And not a sound they make.

The lovely snowflakes cluster
On limbs of naked trees,
Clothing them in dazzling white,
Aided by the gentle breeze.

The snowflakes gently kiss
Cheeks and tip of nose,
Or touch blinking eyelashes
As down to earth they go.

Now maybe the snowflakes
Are angels in disguise,
Only by little children
Are they ever recognized.

Now angel snowflakes
Have no need of wings,
Say the little children
Who seem to know these things.

Bernice Laux

Let justice descend, O heavens, like dew from above,
like gentle rain let the skies drop it down. Let the
earth open and salvation bud forth; let justice also
spring up! I, the Lord, have created this.
Isaiah 45:8

Hold Tight!

Trust Him in the darkness,
'Though bleak and dreary be.
He knows your future, present, past
And what will be, will be.
You cannot ask His reasoning,
He truly has a plan.
Just ride the waves, flow with the tide
And with His patience stand.
Walk along His path in peace
And never give up your faith.
In time you'll find His answer there
And be in His right place.

Ruthmarie Brooks Silver

Loving Friendship

We meet and seem at once to feel
Our hearts and minds respond.
The blessing of God's love within
Cements our friendship bond.

From our treasure of God's love
We share what's in our hearts –
Comfort, warmth and kindness,
And encouraging support.

We stand in faith beside our friend,
Expressing loyalty,
And our optimistic view
Of good, that is to be.

We give our friend a listening ear,
And lend a helping hand...
But most of all we offer
Love, that will understand.

Micky Meyer Mathewson

*The Lord is my strength and
my shield, in whom my heart
trusted and found help. So
my heart rejoices; with my
song I praise my God.*
Psalm 28:7

The Wishing Well

I wished for blue skies,
They turned out grey;
I yearned for tomorrow
While it was still "today."
I wanted dozens of friends
Who were all tried and true;
I looked far and wide
But found only a few.

I dreamed of a future
Where riches abound,
And searched with a vengeance
But nothing I found.
To reach success
Was my life's main goal,
But I climbed the ladder
Without my soul.

Life seemed a failure –
All my dreams were shattered;
Then I met You, Lord,
And nothing else mattered.
Do wishes come true?
Who really can tell?
Yet I found life and hope
At my wishing well.

Eleanor Larson

Awesome

I hear You in the silence,
I hear You in the storm,
I hear You in the baby's cry,
I see You in the dawn.
I feel Your peace each morning
And all throughout the day;
I feel Your peace at bedtime
And every time I pray.
Your awesomeness surrounds me
In everything I do;
How blessed I am to have a God
As wonderful as You.

Frances Gregory Pasch

Soul to Soul

Friends are bonded, soul to soul,
With a special kind of love,
So precious because it is
A blessing from God above.
Friends share a way of thinking,
Good memories from the past,
Experiences in life –
These create the bond that lasts.
Good friends will help each other,
The burdens in life to bear...
Friendship is an expression
Of God's tender loving care.

Steven Michael Schumacher

*Yet there too you shall seek the
Lord, your God; and you shall
indeed find Him when you
search after Him with your
whole heart and your whole soul.*
Deuteronomy 4:29

My strength and my courage is the
Lord, and He has been my Savior.
He is my God, I praise Him; the
God of my father, I extol Him.
Exodus 15:2

Somewhere There's a Rainbow

Though confronted by life's trials,
Though blue skies have turned to grey,
Somewhere there's a rainbow shining
That awaits a perfect day.
When your heart is heavy-laden
And your burdens hard to bear,
God is just a prayer away, friend –
Cast on Him your every care.
In His presence you'll find comfort,
All your heartache He will share;
And you'll find your faith is strengthened
At the blessed throne of prayer.
Though you walk through storm-filled valleys,
And the path ahead grows dim,
God will give you hope and courage
If you place your trust in Him.
Just as there's no cloud above us
That the sunshine can't pierce through,
There's no problem in your life, my friend,
That God can't work out for you.
Some glad day you will awaken
To find dark clouds passed away;
And there, just beyond the rainbow,
There will shine a perfect day.

Beverly J. Anderson

In My Garden

In my flower garden
A bed of pansies grow
And with their brilliant colors,
Their beauty always glows.
Purple and white and yellow they are,
Shining bright as an evening star...
Standing out from all the rest,
I think I like my pansies best.
Yet, there are others I must mention, too...
Red roses drenched with morning dew,
And fragrant wisteria that gracefully drapes
The trees and bushes, resemble grapes.
And around my garden's fence entwines
The delicate blossoms of honeysuckle vines,
Filling the air with sweet perfume...
Oh! Springtime's off to a lovely tune!

Lou Ella Cullipher

God's Gift of Spring

The budding trees, the rainbow's hue,
The brimming tulip cups of dew;
The greening grass, the butterflies,
The picture-perfect sun-kissed skies.
The nesting birds, the daffodils,
The wildflowers dotting distant hills;
The star-kissed skies, the bright moon-glow,
The blooming gifts God does bestow.
The redbud trees, the dogwoods white,
The pungent lilac-perfumed night;
The robin red-breasts on the wing,
These gifts God gives to us each Spring.

Nora M. Bozeman

At dawn may the Lord bestow faithful love
that I may sing praise through the night,
praise to the God of my life.
Psalm 42:9

Twilight in the Garden

When there's silence in the garden
And the breeze is dying down,
When the birds have hushed their singing
And there's stillness all around,
I can feel the mighty presence
Of someone who can't be seen,
Yet I know that He is near me
For I feel His love supreme.

When I'm walking in the garden,
Oft' I pause and linger there
In the softer light of evening,
Bow my head to God in prayer.
And when twilight's in the garden
And multitudes of stars appear,
I'm in awe of God's creation
And I feel His presence near.

When there's twilight in the garden
And flowers' fragrance fills the air,
'Though life's troubles may surround me
I am never in despair,
For I know that God's in Heaven
And is always in control –
My Creator and my Savior –
The Redeemer of my soul.

Luther Elvis Albright

The fig tree puts forth its figs, and the vines, in bloom, give forth fragrance. Arise, my beloved, my beautiful one, and come!

Song 2:13

The Fragrance of Love

The fragrance of love
Is like a sweet smelling flower,
Or the fragrance of rain,
After a Spring shower.
It comes to your heart
In the form of a deed;
Or a kindness that's rendered
For some special need.
You can send out fragrance
Of love every day,
By doing for others,
And not turning away.
No matter how small
A gesture may seem,
The results can be great
When you aid in a dream.
A pleasant smile or handshake,
Or a card in the mail,
Release the fragrance of love,
And true love never fails.

Frances Culpe Wolfe

Welcome one another, then,
as Christ welcomed you,
for the glory of God.
Romans 15:7

98

My Home

My home provides a haven,
When the storms of life are near;
It welcomes me with open arms,
And serves to calm my fears.

My home is somewhere I can do
The things that I like best,
Like read a book or write a while,
Or just sit back and rest.

The largest mansion just won't do,
Nor travel to Paris or Rome;
I just prefer to nestle down
In my favorite place, my home.

Connie J. Kirby

To a Wee Bird

There's a chill in the air,
My wee bird, you must go
To a land that is warm,
Far away from the snow.
Your birdhouse, I fear,
Will look most forlorn;
Know that I'll miss
Your cheerie songs every morn.
When snowflakes must flee
And crocus push through
I'll be watching to see
The first sight of you.
With so many choices,
In case you forget,
A small flag's on your birdhouse,
I'm glad that we met.
Your comrades are gathering,
It's time for goodbye.
God guide and protect you,
My wee bird in the sky.

Kay Hoffman

*If, while walking along, you chance upon a
bird's nest with young birds or eggs in it, in
any tree or on the ground, and the mother
bird is sitting on them, you shall not take
away the mother bird along with her brood.*
Deuteronomy 22:6

Joy Cometh in the Morning

Another world,
Another view,
Someday I'll see
'Twill all be new.

When I awake,
My eyes shall feast
On beauty that
Shall never cease.

Beyond compare,
My eyes behold.
What to our hearts
God's Word has told.

This earthly view
Shall disappear
When I awake
In Heaven's sphere.

A different world
That day I'll find,
A different body,
A different mind.

One thing the same
Shall always be,
My Savior's
Precious love for me.

Helen Gleason

When I Walk With Jesus

When I walk the path with Jesus
There's never need to fear,
For my doubts and worries vanish
And my problems disappear.

When stormy rain clouds threaten
To leave me in dismay,
My path leads to a rainbow
As His goodness clears the way.

I don't need to see His shadow,
Nor His Words of wisdom hear,
To know that He's beside me –
For I feel His love so near.

His arms are always open
To draw me close inside,
And I can find contentment
Where sweet peace and love abide.

Catherine Janssen Irwin

*Guide me in Your truth and teach me, for You
are God my savior. For You I wait all the long
day, because of Your goodness, Lord.*
Psalm 25:5

105

The Lord Watches Over Us

For all you need, pray to the Lord;
And He answers in sweet accord.
From all harm, He keeps you free,
He watches over you and me.

His grace flows from up above,
Keeping us ever in His love.
No matter wherever you may be,
He watches over you and me.

In times of stress, He lifts you up
And offers to you His Holy Cup
In which all sins are set free;
He watches over you and me.

Prayerfully, uplift your eyes
To Him who dwells in the skies;
Direct to Him your frailty –
He watches over you and me.

Dorothy Ivan Manzlak

Autumn Tree

From my window I can see
My very favorite Autumn tree
In reds and browns of every hue;
What a great Artist painted you?

Thank God for eyes that can behold
These lovely shades of rust and gold;
Oh, that my soul could always be
As beautiful for God to see!

Eleanor Larson

Welcome Autumn

Welcome Autumn! Come right in,
My heart's in need of cheer again.
I fear your paint-pots you did spill
As you came tripping o'er the hill –
A tinge of red and gold I see
Where Summer's green is meant to be.
Fat pumpkins in the garden beam,
So glad to see a change of scene.
The grapes are purpling on the vine,
Sweeter than the rarest wine.
Plump red-cheeked apples everywhere
Could win a prize at county fair.
One yellow leaf I do now see
Perhaps, a greeting sent from thee...
Your kind intent is well expressed;
Welcome Autumn! Be thou my guest.

Kay Hoffman

Welcome one another, then, as Christ
welcomed you, for the glory of God.
Romans 15:7

Autumn's Overture

Acorns are falling from the oaks
Abundantly this year,
And the squirrels are in a frenzy,
Now that Autumn is here.
Leaves are falling from the trees
In colors bright and gay,
Now that birds who lived there
Have migrated away.

Now and then some geese fly by
And honk a fond farewell,
And pumpkins are ripe for picking
Over in the farmer's dell.
Dad is making apple cider;
Mom's baking apple pies
And there's a somber, grayish look
In the Autumn skies.

Spiders are busy spinning webs
That collect morning dew,
For soon they will be frosted
When they come into view.
Autumn is Nature's overture
To the holidays we love,
A symphony of simple grace
In praise to God above.

Clay Harrison

Autumn's More Than Just a State of Mind

Autumn's golden days I treasure,
They bring beauty beyond measure;
Leaves of orange, red and gold
Are delightful to behold.
Mums and marigolds debut
Where Summer's lovely roses grew,
Though flitting butterflies depart,
They still linger in my heart.
Fall and beauty go hand-in-hand
In this seasonal wonderland;
So when Autumn comes I find –
She's more than just a state of mind.

Nora M. Bozeman

Discontentment

The sparrow can't soar like a mighty eagle,
The yellow daffodil can't climb like a vine,
The towering oak can't blossom like a wee rose,
But you'll never hear a wimper or a whine.

For humbly the sparrow accepts its limitations,
And the bold daffodil really knows how to shine,
The ancient oak stands so stately and stoic,
'Cause each is unique of its kind.

'Tis a man filled with much discontentment,
Grows envious at another's best,
And fails to count the many God-given blessings
Tucked inside of his very own treasure chest!

Linda C. Grazulis

No longer shall the sun be your light by day,
Nor the brightness of the moon shine upon you
at night; the Lord shall be your light forever,
your God shall be your glory.
Isaiah 60:19

Autumn's Splendor

Changing beauty marks each season
Our spirits to enthrall,
But by far my favorite season
Is when leaves begin to fall.
When Autumn paints the distant hillsides
In crimson, yellow and in gold;
Every garden, every roadside
Depicts brush strokes, bright and bold.
When in wetlands and in meadows
Bush and bramble stands aglow;
And again the blackbirds gather
To fly south before the snow.

When the days are getting shorter,
A chill hangs in the breathless air.
Filled again is barn and garner;
Tranquil fields lie brown and bare.
When the sky is like a sapphire,
Flawless, of the clearest blue.
Mellow sunshine warms the noon day;
Precious days, so still, so few.
As I walk through fields and woodlands,
Dry leaves rustle at my feet.
Oh, the splendor of the season,
Autumn days, so bittersweet.

Regina Wiencek

God's Love Is Ever Near

He guards us through a watchful eye
When dangers lurk as we pass by;
He always has a listening ear
For He can hear each quiet tear;
He comforts with a soothing hand
And lifts us when we cannot stand;
His love consoles us day or night
When our hopes and dreams take flight,
And when this earth we cease to roam,
He'll be the light that leads us home.

Catherine Janssen Irwin

Precious Lord, We Greet Thee

Precious Lord, we greet Thee,
Hear us as we pray.
Grant us strength and wisdom
In all we do and say.
Give us open eyes –
Thy blessings may we see;
And open ears to hear
All needs, where'er they be;
And wash our thoughts with love,
That steadfastly we'll know
We are forgiven, as we forgive,
Let peace forever flow.
Walk beside us now,
Bless us all each day.
Precious Lord, we greet Thee,
Hear us as we pray!

Edna Massimilla

*Go closer, you, and hear all
that the Lord, our God, will
say, and then tell us what the
Lord, our God, tells you; we
will listen and obey.*
Deuteronomy 5:27

Holy Spirit

Come into my heart, Holy Spirit
And please do flood me with Your divine love.
Fall upon my weary, longing soul,
Resembling a heavenly dove.
Fill me with kindness and mercy
As I meet those needy and troubled in soul.
Help me reach out in faith to them,
Shining the Christ, glowing His love so bold.
Come into my life, Holy Spirit
And steer me as You guide me along,
For life is a miraculous journey;
Please lift me and fill me with song.
When I'm depressed and lonely,
Let me feel Your presence nearby,
Making the heavy burdens lighter
As You dry the tears that I cry.

Oh, Holy Spirit, please surround me
As I praise God for His goodness and care,
Lifting me to heights of hope and faith
As I bow humbly in heartfelt prayer.
Be with me, oh Blessed Spirit,
For I trust You to lead the way
O'er hills and valleys and mountaintops,
Revealing God's Holy Will each day!

Linda C. Grazulis

*Sing to God, praise the divine
name; exalt the rider of the
clouds. Rejoice before this God
whose name is the Lord.*
Psalm 68:5

In Winter

In the middle of Winter,
When deep is the ermine snow,
The squirrel lays fast asleep,
Tail wrapped snug about its nose.
And on Winter's coldest day,
Cardinals know where to find
A patch of Summer berries
That the bears have left behind.
Oh, at the heart of Winter,
Springtime's hope is to be found
Within each sleeping seed that
God has planted in the ground.

Steven Michael Schumacher

Nature Helps
the Soul to Heal

Nature helps the soul to heal
When sorrows come to call
From seaside strolls in Summer
To turning leaves in Fall.

An hour in a garden
Can ease a broken heart.
When we stop to smell the roses,
How quickly cares depart.

Every season brings new blessings,
And blessings make us whole,
For Spring brings resurrection
To every weary soul.

From fireflies in clover
To freshly fallen snow,
Creation keeps us humble
Wherever we may go.

When we wish upon a star
Or watch the raindrops fall,
Nature helps the soul to heal
When sorrows come to call.

Clay Harrison

December Days

Remember the days when we counted each one,
Looking forward and wishing for those that would come,
Waiting and hoping to see the first flake,
Tasting cookies that Mama would bake!
All of December, it seemed so long
Until the radio would play each Christmas song,
Seeing the stores all trimmed with light,
Hearing the church bells sound in the night,
Searching the mailbox for cards that brought cheer,
Knowing that family and friends all would be here,
Gathering together on those wonderful days,
Singing old hymns and giving God praise,
Warming our fingers and also our toes,
Holding our scarves on our red and cold nose,
Still loath to go in when we were outdoors at play,
Not wanting the end of a great Winter's day,
Hearing the snow crunch under our feet,
Watching bonfires that gave off such heat,
Sledding down hills was such a delight;
The sounds of our voices rang through the night.
Once again, let's remember that time of the year,
Greet all our friends with love and good cheer.

Milly Patzer

Warmth

The gentle leaves surrender
To the gusting breeze.
The Summer's warmth grows dimmer
With Winter's icy freeze.
As the frigid cold
Engulfs the world outside,
My heart retains its warmth,
For within the Lord resides.

Rebecca Sweeney

When Snowflakes Dance

When snowflakes dance upon the earth
And do their swift routine,
The hills and valleys glisten white
As snowmen dot the scene.

Barren branches sparkle so,
With frozen ice and snow,
'Cause when snowflakes dance upon the earth,
A blizzard oft can blow!

At such times we long for Spring
And flowers rich with bloom,
We also yearn for Autumn's glow,
But not for Winter's chilly gloom.

Yet, with each season that passes by,
We can be sustained
By our faith in the God of love
Who shares our every pain.

So get out and enjoy the snowflakes
As they dance and gently drift,
For God uniquely created every one
To give us such a lift!

Linda C. Grazulis

I Said a Prayer for You Today

I said a prayer for you today
And thought you'd like to know
How much your friendship means to me
Wherever I may go.
You hold a very special place
Enshrined within my heart.
Your hugs transform my darkest days
Into a work of art.

You sense the pain I try to hide
And know just what to say.
You lift me up each time I fall
And wipe my tears away.
I said a prayer for you today
As you have done for me
More times than I could ever count
Through years that ceased to be.

We can't always be together
And yet I know you're there,
For when I need my special friend,
You come to me through prayer.
We've shared the ups and downs of life
And helped each other grow.
I said a prayer for you today
And thought you'd like to know.

Clay Harrison

For then you shall delight in the
Almighty and you shall lift up
your face toward God.
Job 22:26

Forgive

Dear Lord, I would forgive those
Who often hurt my pride,
And leave my spirit broken
With hurt I cannot hide.
I realize that Thou has taught
To turn the other cheek;
Although this works for others,
I find that I am weak.
Dear God, please help me grow in grace
That as each day I live,
To never find within my heart
A wrong I can't forgive.

Anna Lee Edwards McAlpin